eyewonder

Bugs

DK

Project Editor Upamanyu Das
Project Art Editor Noopur Dalal
Editor Shahid Qureshi
Illustrator Aparajita Sen
Picture Researcher Ridhima Sikka
Managing Editor Kingshuk Ghoshal
Managing Art Editors Anna Hall, Govind Mittal
Pre-production Team Mohammad Rizwan, Bimlesh Tiwary
Production Editor Anita Yadav
Production Controller Jack Matts
Project Jackets Art Editor Vidushi Chaudhry
India Creative Head Malavika Talukder
Associate Publisher Gemma Farr
Art Director Mabel Chan

Consultant Prof Adam Hart

This edition published in 2026
First published in Great Britain in 2002 by
Dorling Kindersley Limited
20 Vauxhall Bridge Road,
London, SW1V 2SA

The authorised representative in the EEA is
Dorling Kindersley Verlag GmbH. Arnulfstr. 124,
80636 Munich, Germany

Copyright © 2002, 2015, 2026 Dorling Kindersley Limited
A Penguin Random House Company
10 9 8 7 6 5 4 3 2 1
001–354831–Apr/2026

All rights reserved.
No part of this publication may be reproduced, stored in or introduced into a retrieval system, or transmitted, in any form, or by any means (electronic, mechanical, photocopying, recording, or otherwise), without the prior written permission of the copyright owner.
DK values and supports copyright. Thank you for respecting intellectual property laws by not reproducing, scanning or distributing any part of this publication by any means without permission. By purchasing an authorised edition, you are supporting writers and artists and enabling DK to continue to publish books that inform and inspire readers. No part of this publication may be used or reproduced in any manner for the purpose of training artificial intelligence technologies or systems. In accordance with Article 4(3) of the DSM Directive 2019/790, DK expressly reserves this work from the text and data mining exception.

A CIP catalogue record for this book
is available from the British Library.
ISBN: 978-0-2417-7737-4

Printed and bound in China

www.dk.com

This book was made with Forest Stewardship Council™ certified paper – one small step in DK's commitment to a sustainable future.
Learn more at www.dk.com/uk/information/sustainability

Contents

4-5
A bug's life

6-7
Leapers and creepers

8-9
Up, up, and away

10-11
Making sense

12-13
Meat eaters

14-15
No meat for us!

16-17
Now you see me

18-19
Warning signals

20-21
Bug parents

22-23
Growing up

24-25
What's the buzz?

26-27
Little soldiers

28-29
Forest dwellers

30-31
Dry deserts

32-33
Water world

34-35
House mates

36-37
After dark

38-39
Body basics

40-41
Little pests

42-43
Cleaning up

44-45
Brilliant bugs

46-47
Bug patrol

48-49
Honey trail

50-51
Who am I?

52-53
First flight

54-55
Glossary and Animal alphabet

56
Index and Acknowledgments

A bug's life

The tiny animals we call bugs can be found nearly everywhere on Earth – there are more than a million different types! They fly through the air, swim through water, crawl on land, or dig down into the ground.

Trapped in time
Bugs have been around for more than 400 million years. Scientists have found ancient bugs trapped inside amber (tree sap that has hardened over time).

Segmented bodies
Arthropods are a group of tiny animals with hard outer skeletons and bodies made of segments. Some types of arthropods are also called bugs. They include insects.

Head
Thorax
Abdomen

An insect, such as this goliath beetle, has six legs and a body made of three parts.

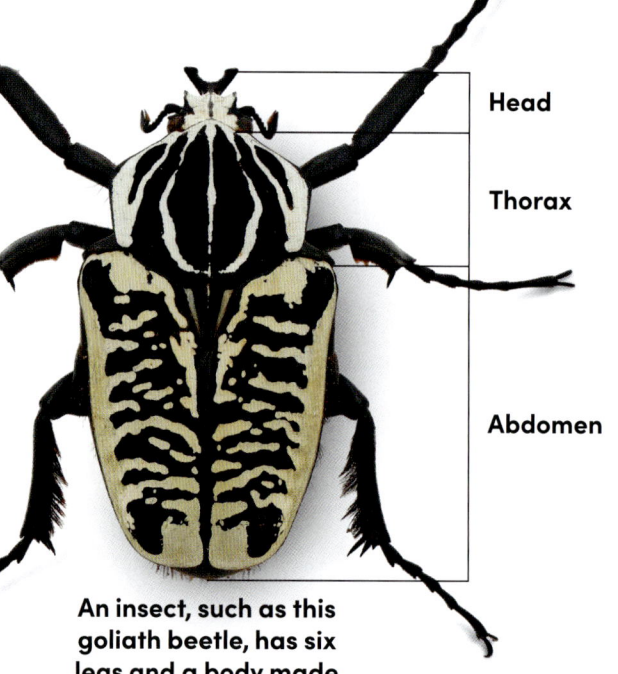

Mexican red-knee tarantula, a spider

Eight-legged wonders
Spiders and scorpions are also examples of bugs. They have eight legs and bodies that are divided into two parts.

Many-legged marchers

If you try counting the legs on a bug and you find you can't, the chances are you are looking at a many-legged bug called a myriapod, such as a millipede or a centipede.

Indian tiger centipede

Centipedes have a pair of legs on each section of their body.

Fast facts

Bugs outnumber humans by more than a billion to one.

Insects were thriving before the age of dinosaurs.

Scientists believe that only a fraction of the world's insect species have been discovered.

A bright green colour helps this jewel bug hide among leaves.

Incredible insects

Bugs, such as insects, have the same basic body parts, but they come in a huge range of colours, shapes, and sizes.

Jewel bug, an insect found mostly in Southeast Asia

A sea of legs
Millipedes have two pairs of legs on most sections of their long bodies. Some of them have 400 legs, but the record-holder has more than 1,300 legs!

North America's black and orange millipede walks on around 60 legs.

Leapers and creepers

Some bugs are speedy, some are slow. Some run and others jump. How they move around depends on where they live and what they face.

High jumper
The flea has strong back legs that let it spring really high into the air. Some fleas can jump 200 times their body length. This is like a person jumping over the Eiffel Tower in France, which is 300 m (984 ft) high!

Cat flea leaps into the air.

The grippers at the back of the caterpillar are called "prolegs".

The caterpillar's prolegs grip the twig tightly.

Leaping away
If a grasshopper or cricket is disturbed and it needs to get away, it uses its muscle-packed legs to leap high into the air.

Meadow grasshopper

Front to back
Caterpillars are the larvae (young ones) of butterflies or moths. When walking on twigs, they stretch their body forwards, arch up their back, then pull their back end to the front.

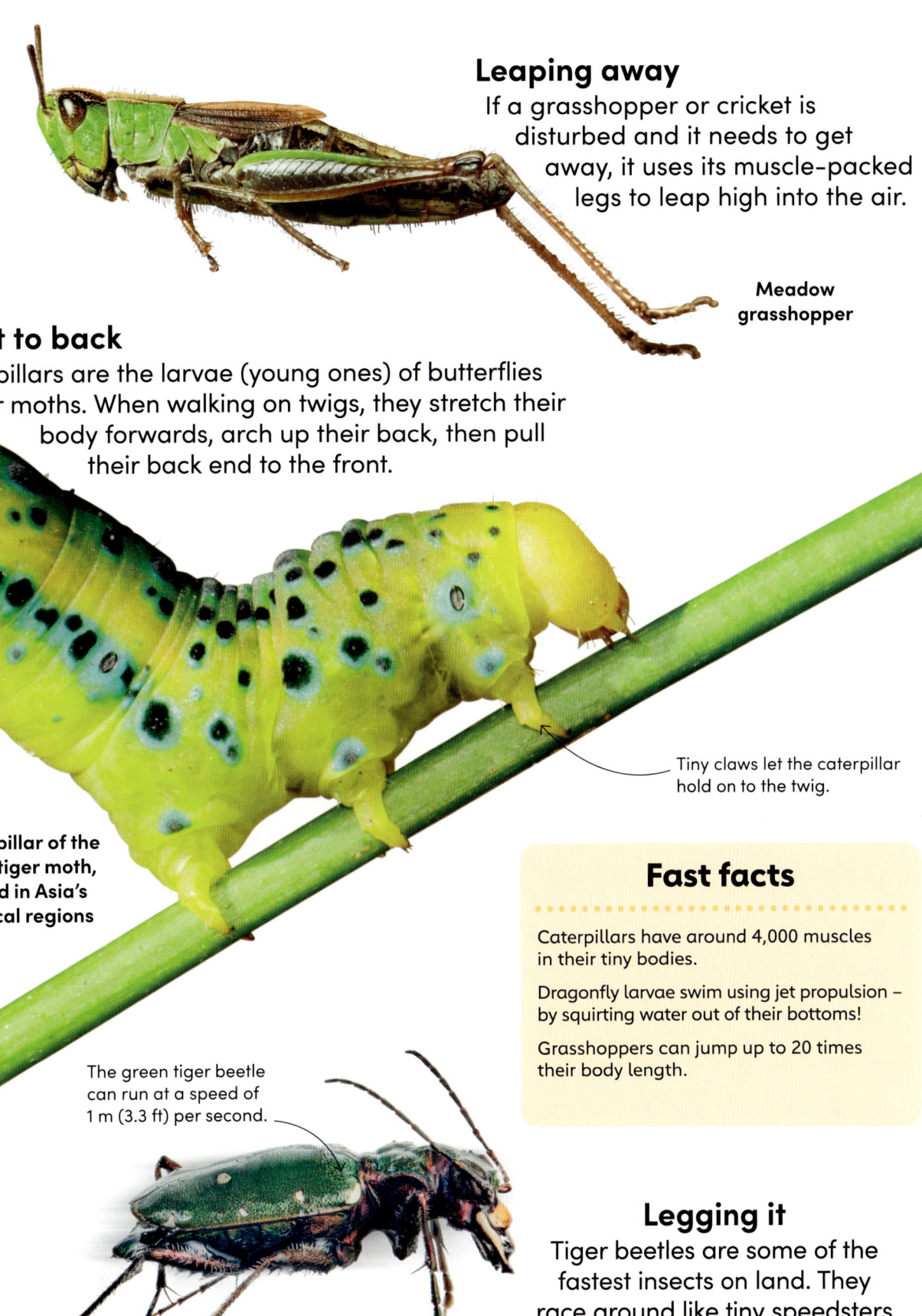

Tiny claws let the caterpillar hold on to the twig.

Caterpillar of the false tiger moth, found in Asia's tropical regions

Fast facts
Caterpillars have around 4,000 muscles in their tiny bodies.

Dragonfly larvae swim using jet propulsion – by squirting water out of their bottoms!

Grasshoppers can jump up to 20 times their body length.

The green tiger beetle can run at a speed of 1 m (3.3 ft) per second.

Legging it
Tiger beetles are some of the fastest insects on land. They race around like tiny speedsters when chasing food or running away from predators.

Taking to the air

Flying insects flap their wings to fly, but different species may do it in different ways. Dragonflies flap their wings one after the other. Butterflies flap their four wings together, often many times a second.

Ithomiine butterfly, found in Central and South America

Aerial acrobats

Lacewings can control each pair of wings separately, which means they can turn easily when flying.

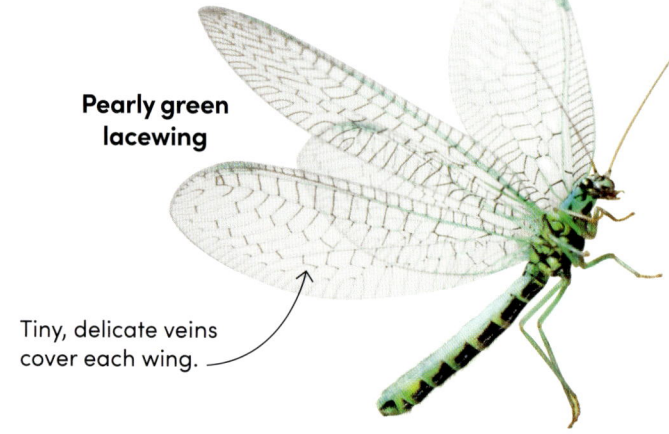

Pearly green lacewing

Tiny, delicate veins cover each wing.

Gone in a flash!

The marmalade hoverfly can beat its wings up to 1,000 times in a second. It hovers in the air, then darts away.

 MIGRATING MONARCHS

Millions of monarch butterflies migrate (travel thousands of kilometres) across North America every year. They do this to escape the cold winter and to find food. The journey is so long that individual butterflies don't survive the whole way – it takes many generations to complete the migration.

Balancing act
The second set of wings on a crane fly look like small, club-shaped sticks, called halteres. The insect uses these to balance itself when flying.

Halteres of a crane fly

Unmoving front wings

Armoured wings
The common red soldier beetle has two pairs of wings but uses only one pair to fly. Its front wings have become leathery cases that protect the flying wings when they are folded away.

The soldier beetle has a nickname: leatherwings.

Up, up, and away

Bugs are the ultimate explorers – they can get anywhere and everywhere. Many of them are expert fliers, who use their pairs of wings to zip off in search of food or to make a daring escape from predators.

Making sense

Imagine being able to taste with your feet, or having eyes as big as your head! Bugs have the same senses as we do, but many of them also have unusual body parts which help them to find out more about their surroundings.

Feeling the way
A cave cricket can be found hanging out in moist, cool, and dark places, such as caves and basements. It has poor eyesight, so it uses its antennae, or "feelers", to get around without hitting walls.

Eyes everywhere
Male mayflies have seven eyes! Some even have a pair on top of the head to help them look for females flying overhead. The three in the front detect light, and the two on the side let these insects see around their body.

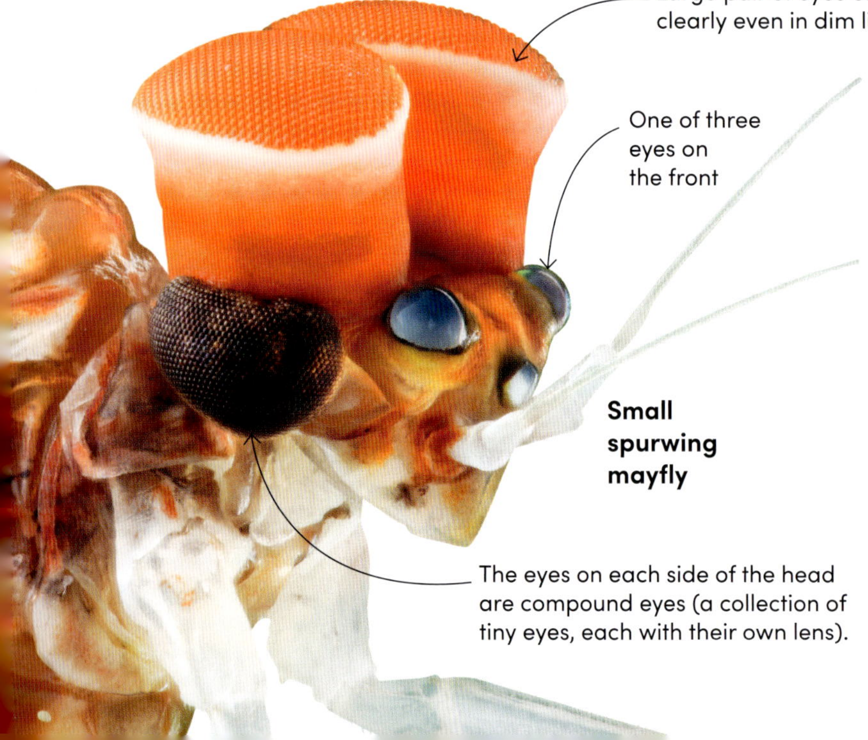

Large pair of eyes can see clearly even in dim light.

One of three eyes on the front

Small spurwing mayfly

The eyes on each side of the head are compound eyes (a collection of tiny eyes, each with their own lens).

Taste sensors on a butterfly's feet can tell if a plant is poisonous.

Listen up
We hear sounds using ears on our head, but bugs can catch sounds using different parts of their body. This katydid (bush-cricket) can listen with its knees!

Super sniffer
Antennae are also used to smell. This male Indian moon moth has two hairy antennae that can smell a female from 11 km (6.8 miles) away!

Slits above the knees can "hear" calls made by other crickets.

Great green bush-cricket

A matter of taste
Some butterflies taste with their feet. When this eastern tiger swallowtail lands on a particularly tasty flower, its long, hollow tongue, or proboscis, unfolds to let it drink nectar.

Meat eaters

There are so many bugs that eat other bugs, you would have thought it would be easy for predators to catch and eat prey. Wrong! Hunters have to invent cunning ways to get their dinner, and some have special ways to eat it, too.

Little suckers
The assassin bug pierces the body of its prey to inject its saliva. This turns the prey's insides to liquid, which the assassin bug then sucks out.

Underwater terror
Great diving beetles are fast and formidable predators, lurking in many ponds in Europe and Asia. They hunt any pond dwellers they can catch, even tadpoles and fish!

Fast facts

Dragonflies are some of the most effective hunters. They almost always catch their prey!

Ladybirds hunt aphids, which eat plants. This makes them useful to gardeners.

Spiders are sneaky predators. Most of them spin webs made of silk to snare insects when hunting for food.

Wrap it up

When a bug flies into a spider's web, the spider wraps it up in silk to stop it from moving. Then the spider injects it with venom, before sucking out its insides.

The praying mantis is killed by the venom before being eaten.

Night hunter

Most centipedes hunt living prey, usually at night. The Tanzanian blue ring-legged centipede (right) injects venom into its prey with a special pair of fangs.

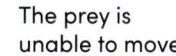
The prey is unable to move.

Speedy striker

A praying mantis sits still among leaves with its forelegs ready to strike. When an insect passes, it pounces at lightning speed.

Prey caught between the mantis's strong, spiky front legs

Caterpillars eat a lot to grow fast.

Painted lady butterfly

A butterfly uses its proboscis (long, hollow tongue) to suck nectar from a flower.

No meat for us!

Many bugs love their veggies. They eat leaves, flowers, and nectar. Their mouths match the food they eat: some pierce and suck, others bite and chew.

Feeding frenzy
Caterpillars are big eaters. The caterpillars of the dusky birch sawfly have strong teeth for chewing through tough leaves.

Liquid lunch
Once the caterpillar of a butterfly turns into an adult, its diet changes. It now feeds only on liquids.

👁 BUGS BEWARE!
It's not just bugs that eat plants – some plants eat bugs! These plants are called carnivorous plants. One of them is this Venus flytrap. It has caught a grasshopper in one of its spiky leaves.

Leaf-cutter ants can lift up to 50 times their body weight.

Nuts about nuts
The acorn weevil loves eating acorns in oak forests. It pierces each nut with its long snout. Then it uses the jaws at the end of the snout to chew away at the inside of the nut.

Fungi farmers
Leaf-cutter ants cut sections of leaves to carry back to their nest. They use them to grow a type of fungus, which is their food.

Praying mantises come in many colours.

The mantis waits patiently to catch prey.

Blending in
The orchid mantis looks a lot like the flower it is named after. It can be pink or white, to blend in with the flowers it sits on.

Now you see me

Lurking in the undergrowth are many bugs. Cunning ways of blending into their surroundings, or camouflages, help some bugs to catch a meal and others to avoid becoming one.

Katydids are found in tropical and subtropical forests around the world.

Is that a stick?
Stick insects are so well camouflaged that at first glance they look just like sticks. Until the insect moves, it's hard to tell if it's a twig or a bug.

The butterfly perches with its wings spread wide.

Master of disguise
Brown mottled patterns cover the grey cracker butterfly's wings, making it hard to spot against tree bark.

Spiky survivors
Treehopper bugs disguise themselves as spiky thorns. This helps keep them safe – even hungry birds are unlikely to risk landing on a prickly branch!

Lost among leaves
The leaf-mimic katydid has the perfect disguise. It hides in plain sight among the bright green leaves. It even has veins, just as in real leaves.

Snake scare

It may look like a snake, but this is actually a caterpillar of a sphinx hawk moth. It cleverly mimics a snake to escape hunters.

Warning signals

Some bugs make it obvious to their attackers that they would be nasty if eaten. Others have methods that startle hunters, and a few use clever disguises.

Defensive display

When attacked, the puss moth caterpillar rears up its colourful head. Bright colours warn predators that a bug is poisonous, so they leave it alone.

Hot bomb

When it feels threatened, a bombardier beetle squirts a chemical out of its bottom at high speed, at a temperature of nearly 100°C (212°F)!

Making eyes

Imagine stumbling across a Polyphemus moth in a North American forest. You'd think that those "eyes" were on a much bigger and more ferocious animal.

Wētā whack

You might spot an enormous wētā cricket in New Zealand's forests. Disturb one and you are in for a shock. Quick as a flash, it shoots its back legs up to give a sharp kick.

The bug waves the pink ends of its tail to ward off predators.

Viceroy butterfly, found across North America

Copycat bug

Some bugs are lazy. They are not harmful, but they copy the colours of something that is, so they are left alone. Predators such as birds can't tell apart the delicious Viceroy butterfly from the foul-tasting Monarch.

Monarch butterfly, found commonly in North, Central, and South America

Defender mum
The female cotton harlequin bug stands guard over her eggs, to protect them from predators. Once they hatch, she stays with them for a number of weeks.

Orange female with green and purple young ones on a hibiscus tree

Fast facts

Only around 1 per cent of insects show any parental care for their eggs and young. In most cases, the adult female is the involved parent.

Earwig mothers lick their eggs clean, to stop fungi growing on them.

Among the giant water bugs, it is the male that looks after the eggs. He cleans them regularly, and often carries them around until they hatch.

A heavy load
The female wolf spider carries her eggs around on her back. Once the baby spiders hatch, they climb back up, and are carried around for several weeks.

Bug parents

Most bugs lay their eggs and then leave them. But some types of bugs might stay with their eggs to protect them, or feed their babies once they hatch.

Mega meal

The parasitic wasp lays its eggs on a live caterpillar, which can't shake them off. The caterpillar keeps getting bigger until the wasp larvae hatch out and gobble it up!

Wasp eggs attached by silken threads to a butterfly caterpillar in a rainforest in Ecuador

Protective shield

A mother shield bug uses her body as a shield against predators. She leads her young to the plants they will need to eat.

A shield bug mum stands over her larvae in a Japanese woodland.

1 Life begins
Butterflies begin life as eggs. The female lime butterfly lays a single egg on a leaf of a tree.

2 Eating to grow
The egg hatches into a small, hairy caterpillar. It eats and eats, getting steadily bigger.

Caterpillar

Growing up

Insects start their lives as eggs. Some look very different from their adult form, changing how they look as they grow. This is called complete metamorphosis. Others barely change, or do so more slowly, from egg to adult.

LOOKALIKES

When silverfish nymphs (young ones) hatch out of eggs, they look similar to their adult form. They do get bigger, growing a little larger each time they moult (shed their skin).

Silverfish nymph

Adult silverfish

Skip a stage
Some insects, such as this desert locust from Asia, become adults without the pupa stage in between. The nymph changes a bit each time it sheds its skin, turning into an adult.

Shed skin

Freshly moulted desert locust

3 Time for change

The caterpillar sheds its skin, becoming a pupa. Its body changes shape inside the pupa.

4 Out you come

Once the new butterfly is fully formed, the pupa splits open. The butterfly climbs out and dries its wings.

5 Taking flight

The adult butterfly looks completely different to its caterpillar stage. It is now ready to fly off and find a mate.

Once it is large enough, the caterpillar anchors itself to the tree branch with silk.

THE WAGGLE

When bees come across a good source of nectar, they perform a special "waggle" dance to tell other bees about it. The more times a bee waggles, the further away the food is.

The bee moves in a figure of eight.

It waggles its tail in the middle of the dance.

Housing honey

Honeybees build layers of honeycomb using wax they make. These have holes – some protect growing bee larvae. Others contain honey, which the bees make from flower nectar.

What's the buzz?

If you hear a buzzing sound in your garden, chances are you are listening to something that stings, such as a bee or wasp. In many of these insects, the females work together in groups, building delicate structures to house and feed their young.

Making honey
Bees collect pollen and nectar from flowers. The nectar is then passed back and forth between bees' mouths, turning it into honey.

Bees carry pollen between flowers, helping the plants grow seeds.

A growing home
The queen wasp starts the nest by chewing dead wood, mixing it with saliva, and letting it dry. She then lays some eggs. After hatching, the next generation continues the nest-building.

Some wasps live in large paper nests.

Sweet tooth
All wasps love sweet fruits. That's why they buzz around your food in the summer. They won't sting unless you threaten them.

Firm friends

Ants and aphids keep each other happy. The aphids eat a lot of tree sap and give off a sweet liquid that the ants like to sip. In return, the ants protect them from predators.

Network of tunnels

The queen's chamber is at the centre of the mound.

Termite tower

Some species of termites live in huge mounds that they build using soil, saliva, and their poo. The mounds can be up to 6 m (20 ft) high.

👁 A BRIDGE OF BODIES

Weaver ants live on trees in the tropical forests of Asia, Australia, and the Pacific. They can link together to form bridges that helps them cross the gaps between trees.

Weaver ants defend their leafy nests against intruders by spraying acid from their abdomen.

Tiny builders
Some ants build nests of leaves. They each carry an ant larva in their jaws and make it produce silk, which they then use to sew up the leaves.

A colony of weaver ants in the tropical rainforests of the Andaman Islands, India

Little soldiers

Ants and termites live in colonies in which everyone works together. Each insect has its own job. The queen lays eggs, while others work as nursemaids, guards, builders, and food gatherers.

Moon moth
The Madagascan moon moth flutters through the rainforests of Madagascar, Africa. It lives as an adult for around five days, and doesn't eat at all during this time.

This moth can whirl its tails to confuse predators such as bats.

Forest dwellers

The rainforest is home to bugs of all shapes and sizes. Nobody knows quite how many species there are in the forest, as scientists find new ones all the time.

Fast facts

The Amazon Rainforest is home to more than 2.5 million different insect species.

More than 3,600 kinds of spiders live in the Amazon Rainforest, many of which can't be found anywhere else in the world!

Male Madagascan moon moths have longer tails than females.

This centipede can grow as long as 25 cm (10 in).

Fast and fierce
Bugs and even frogs and mice are not safe from the Vietnamese giant centipede as it hunts prey on the forest floor.

Hairy hunter
The Costa Rican red-leg tarantula is named for the orange-red tufts on its hairy legs. It sleeps through the day in its silk-lined underground burrow, emerging at night to hunt for large insects.

Stinger to inject a deadly chemical called venom into prey

A waxy coating on this scorpion's body helps it retain water.

The female stings her prey, which stops it from moving.

Sting of death
The female emerald jewel wasp will sting a cockroach, drag it into its sandy burrow, and lay an egg on it. Its larva (young one) will eat the cockroach when it hatches.

Sand survivor
Africa's Kalahari Desert is home to the Cape burrowing scorpion. This hunter hardly ever needs to drink. It gets most of its moisture from bugs it eats.

Full of nectar

Some honeypot ants fill their tummies with nectar until they swell up like balloons. When food is short, the ants with the swollen tummies vomit up the nectar to feed it to others in their colony.

Dew collects on the beetle's legs.

Dew drinker

The darkling beetle has a clever way of quenching its thirst in the Namib Desert of southern Africa. It waits until the morning when dew has formed on its back, then leans forwards to let the dew trickle into its mouth.

Honeypot ant in a desert in Arizona, USA

👁 BUGS ON ICE

Some bugs can survive in very cold places. Ice crawlers flourish on mountains and at the edges of glaciers (slow-moving rivers of snow), in temperatures just above freezing.

Dry deserts

The desert can be tough for many plants and animals. Only the cleverest bugs can live in this dry environment with little or no water.

31

Upside down

The backswimmer hangs upside down just below the surface of the water. It uses its long, oarlike legs to dart around, hunting for smaller insects, tadpoles, and fish.

Walking on water

Pond skaters skim over the water surface. Their feet can sense tiny movements in the water, which lead them towards prey.

Common pond skater on a pond in Wiltshire, UK

Master builder

The larva (young one) of the caddis fly spins sticky silk to bind together stones, shells, and pieces of plants. It uses this case to protect itself.

Water world

A body of water may be filled with very tiny animals – but you may have to look closely to see some of them. Many bugs live in, or above, the water and some can even walk on its surface.

Making bubbles

The diving bell spider lives in water, but it needs to breathe air. This clever bug weaves a web underwater and fills it with air from the surface. This air bubble is its very own air supply!

This spider lives in many ponds and lakes in Europe and Asia.

Lifting off

Dragonflies lay their eggs in water – this is where their larvae hatch. Before becoming an adult, a larva crawls on to a plant stem above the water, sheds its skin, and prepares to use its wings.

A silverfish loves to feed on paper and books.

Hidden silver
Silverfish are shiny, wingless insects. They hide in dark, cool places, such as bookshelves, coming out to find food at night.

House mates

Bugs live all over our homes – in dark corners, in carpets, and even between the pages of our books. Most house-living bugs are completely harmless.

Roach rampage
Cockroaches are not welcome visitors. They eat anything they can find, such as bread, and are very difficult to get rid of once they have settled in.

Fast facts

Carpet moths eat anything with keratin (the substance hair and nails are made of). That includes leather and wool carpets.

Many flies lay their eggs in rotting food. Big swarms of flies can appear once the larvae grow up!

Woodworms (larvae of wood-boring beetles) can eat through wooden furniture and buildings.

Mite menace
Millions of dust mites live in mattresses, furnishings, and carpets inside our homes. We can't see these tiny creatures, but they can cause people to sneeze and wheeze.

House spider
The Adanson's house jumper hides in dark places in your home, such as down a plug hole. You may spot it scuttling across the floor to catch flies and other bugs.

This net-casting spider is ready with its fatal net in a tropical rainforest in Madagascar.

After dark

When the Sun goes down, some insects are just starting to wake up. For many bugs, the night is when they are most active, whether they are getting ready for a meal or avoiding becoming a meal themselves.

Catching dinner
The net-casting spider weaves its web before dark. At night, it waits patiently to drop the web on unsuspecting prey.

Light fantastic
Fireflies are a type of beetle. Like all fireflies, the Japanese firefly uses an organ called a lantern to create flashing light signals. This allows it to talk to others of its kind at night.

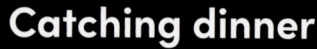

Shiny traps
Cave glow-worms are the larvae of a type of fly. They live in dark, wet places, and produce light to attract prey and mucus to trap it.

Strands of mucus dangle from the glow-worm's body.

Elephant hawk moth feeds on the nectar of a honeysuckle flower in the UK.

Colour in the dark
The elephant hawk moth is one of the few animals that can see colour at night. This skill comes in handy when looking for the best flowers for drinking nectar.

Fast facts

Flap-footed bugs have big flaps on their rear legs, which the males use to attract females.

A dracula ant can close its jaws at 324 kph (201 mph) – more than 2,781 times faster than the blink of an eye!

Body basics

Bugs come in a huge range of shapes and sizes. Some of them may look strange to us, but their bodies are suited to where they live and how they find food.

A spiny devil bush-cricket looks out for prey in the Tiputini rainforest in Ecuador.

Slicing jaws make this cricket a fierce predator.

Barbed body

The spiny devil bush-cricket lives in the Amazon Rainforest. Its head and legs are covered with sharp protective spines. They also help it in catching prey.

Shiny thief

The cuckoo wasp's body gleams with green and blue. It lays its eggs in a nest that belongs to a bee or other wasp. When its eggs hatch, its larvae (young ones) eat all the food and even other larvae!

Cuckoo wasps cannot sting like other wasps.

Stick your neck out

Giraffe weevils have incredibly long necks. The males have necks two or three times longer than the females.

The antennae and head are perched on the end of the long neck.

Stalk-eyed fly on a leaf in Vietnam

Eye contest

Stalk-eyed flies have eyes on stalks on the head. Males compete for females by comparing their eyes with each other. The winner will be the male with the eyes that are furthest apart.

39

Little pests

Bugs may be small, but some of them can do huge damage in large numbers, or even on their own. They can eat whole fields of crops and spread diseases, and can be hard to stop.

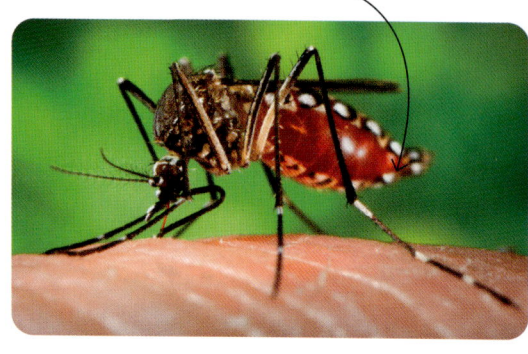

The mosquito's abdomen is swollen with blood.

Tiny trouble
A mosquito is a flying bug found around the world. Female mosquitoes bite other animals to suck their blood. Some can spread dangerous diseases, such as malaria.

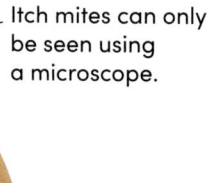

Itch mites can only be seen using a microscope.

Invisible itch
Itch mites are bugs that live on our skin. They are too tiny to be seen with our eyes. They cause itching and soreness.

Hungry locusts
A swarm of billions of locusts can blot out the Sun when flying, and eat every grain of crop in an area in just hours. This swarm is flying over a farm in Meru, Kenya.

Plants in peril

Red spider mites are spiders that suck the sap out of leaves. A large group of these mites can weaken a plant so much that it may die.

A swollen body means a good blood meal.

Blood-thirsty bugs

Ticks feed on blood. They latch on to any animal they can find. While feeding, they can pass along germs that cause disease.

Red spider mites are found commonly in many dry areas.

Locusts can travel up to 145 km (90 miles) a day.

Cleaning up

Some bugs feed on dead plants, animals, and dung. Left uneaten, the remains would build up into a huge stinking pile. Our world would be a lot smellier without these tiny cleaners!

Maggot mayhem
Flies lay their eggs in the rotting meat of a dead animal. Their larvae (young ones) are called maggots. When they hatch, they burrow into the flesh to eat it.

Rolling dung
When a fresh pile of dung (animal poo) appears on the ground, some male dung beetles roll the poo into balls before burying them. Female beetles lay an egg in each ball. When the larvae hatch, they eat the dung.

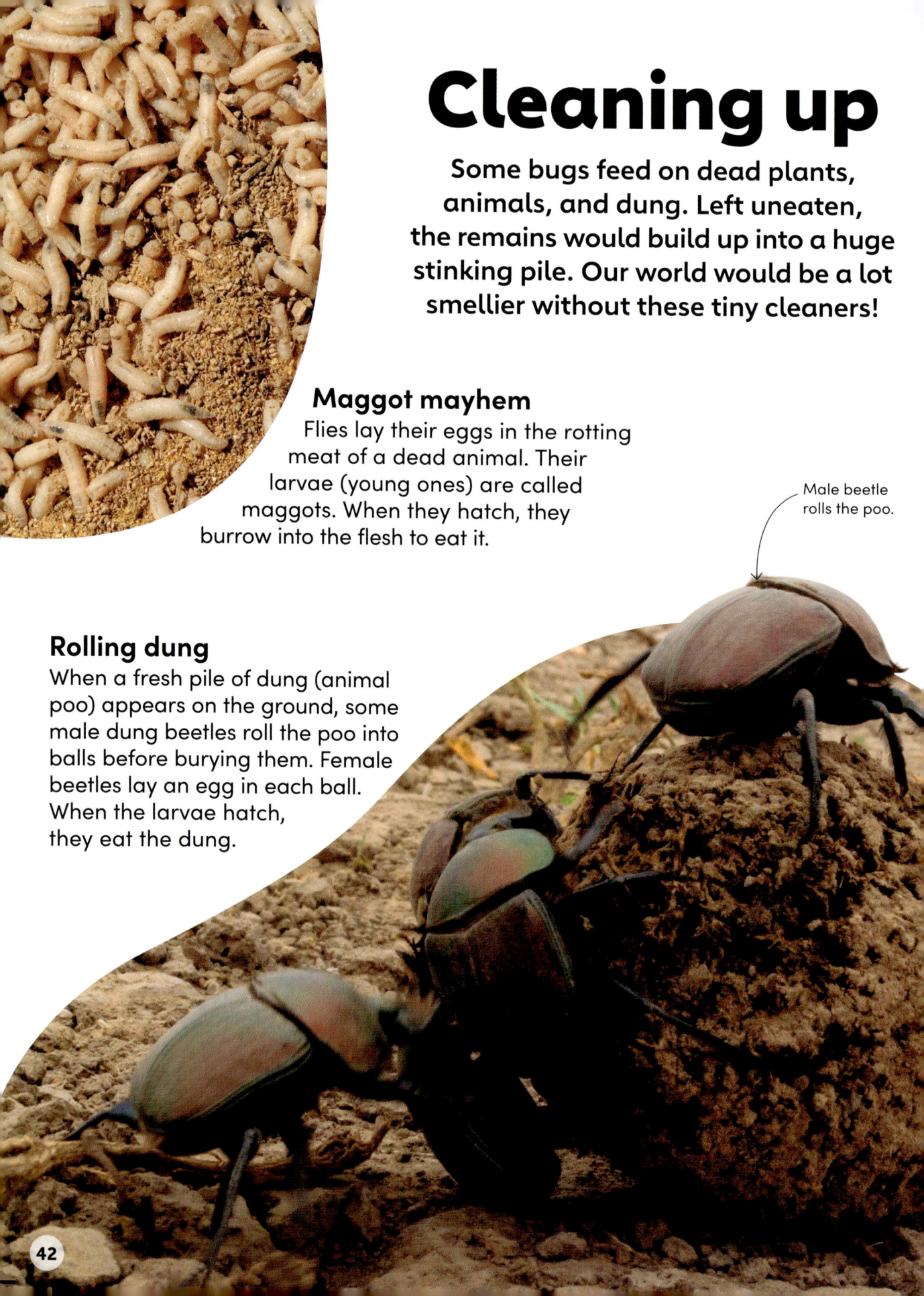

Male beetle rolls the poo.

Burying beetles

Sexton beetles bury the dead bodies of animals such as mice and bats, and lay their eggs on them. When the larvae hatch out of these eggs, they eat away the buried animals, keeping the world above tidy.

Sexton beetles are common in the woodlands of England.

Mini munchers

Earwigs feed on parts of plants as well as spiders and other bugs. They also eat dead leaves and twigs, which keeps plants clean and healthy.

Dung beetles may fight over fresh dung.

👁 ANT BURIALS

Ants live together in huge groups, which means there will always be a few dead ones around. Red ants bury their dead in chosen spots outside their nest, to keep it clean!

Red ant carries away a dead one.

Helping plants

Ants live underground. Their poo improves the soil, helping plants grow. The tunnels they dig allow water and air to reach growing plant roots.

Saving crops

Some insects eat away at food crops. Instead of poisoning them and the crop, farmers get rid of them by bringing in other insects that eat the pests and leave the crop alone.

Harvester ant workers burrow through soil.

A pink-spotted lady beetle (left) eats the eggs of a Colorado potato beetle, a pest.

Brilliant bugs

Bugs help other animals and plants every day! Some bugs eat other harmful ones. Others carry pollen between plants and even keep the soil healthy.

Plant pollinators
Many insects help plants by carrying pollen from flower to flower. This is called pollination, and it helps the plants to produce seeds and make more plants.

Pollen on the legs of a honeybee

Wood warden
Flat dark beetles can be red, yellow, or brown. They feed on the larvae (young ones) of other insects such as bark beetles that damage wood.

On the hunt
Dragonflies are fierce predators. They whizz through the air near rivers and ponds, catching pests such as mosquitoes and moths.

Insect prey

Bug patrol

Around the world, many bugs are dying out because of harmful chemicals called pesticides, the loss of their homes and habitats, and the changing climate. Small actions can make a big difference in the lives of bugs!

Think flowers!
Try to plant flowers that grow locally. These will be the right sort of flowers to provide pollen for local bees and butterflies.

Keep it dark
Artificial lights can confuse insects at night. Try to turn off outdoor lights, or keep them as dim as possible.

Keep it messy
Logs, stones, and long grass offer bugs places to hide and lay their eggs. Try to keep these features in parts of your garden.

Learn about bugs

Try to learn more about the bugs around you. It's fun to know which bug is which! You could read a book or ask an adult to help you search for bugs on the internet.

Making compost

Composting food waste gives insects that eat rotting plants a place to live and food to eat. Once the food has rotted down, it can be used to improve the soil for the other plants in your garden.

Water, water

Bugs need water to drink but can drown in deep water. You can leave water out for them in a shallow dish, with pebbles in the water for bugs to rest on.

Honey trail

A honeybee is trying to return home after collecting nectar. Help it fly through this maze of clues so it can get home fast!

A honeycomb is full of
See page 24

- Water
- Holes
- Stones

When bees find a good nectar supply, they
See page 24

- Laugh
- Sing
- Dance

Bees collect nectar from
See page 25

- Leaves
- Flowers
- Fruits

Start

48

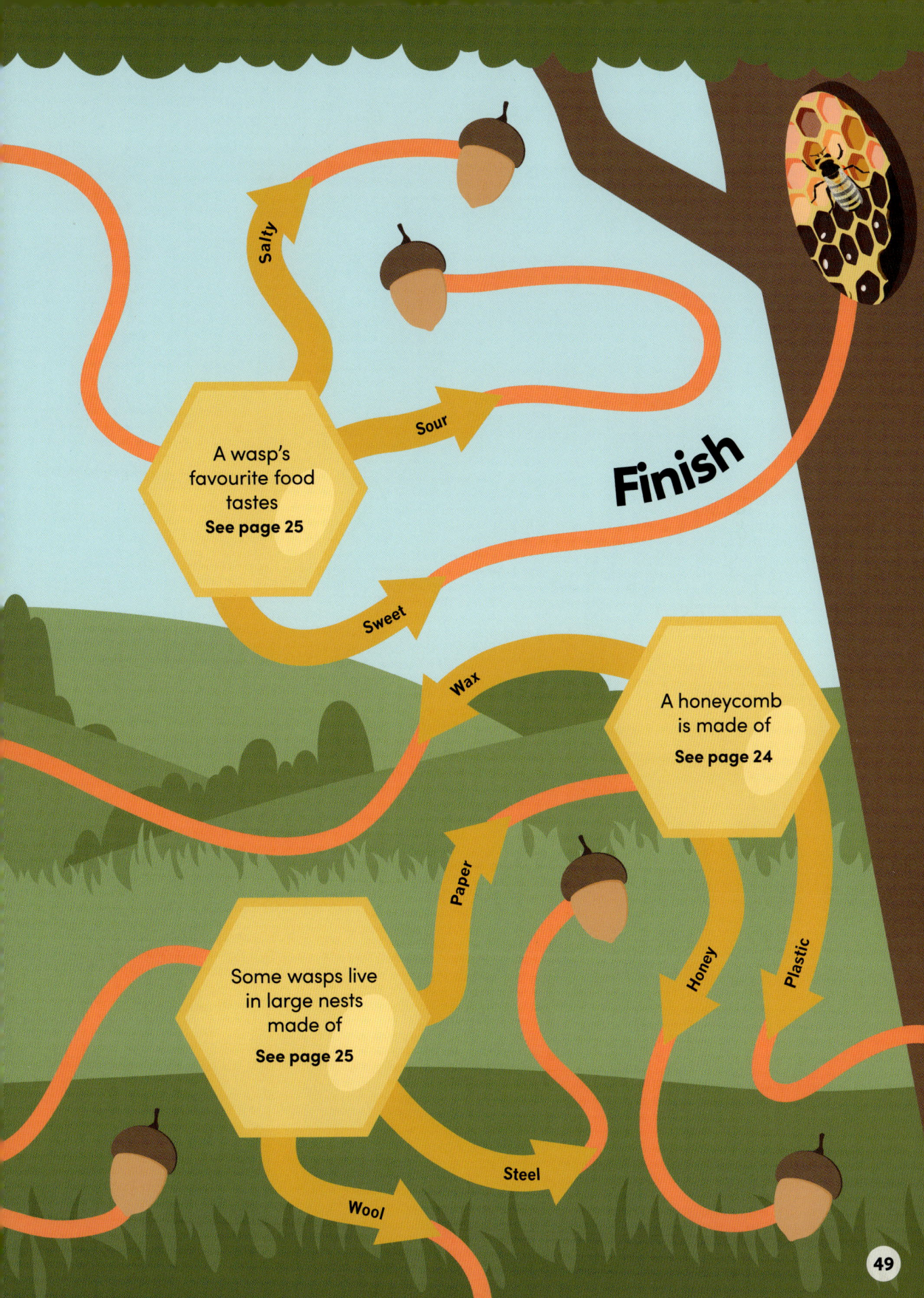

Who am I?

Take a look at these close-ups of bugs in the book, and see if you can identify them. The clues should help you!

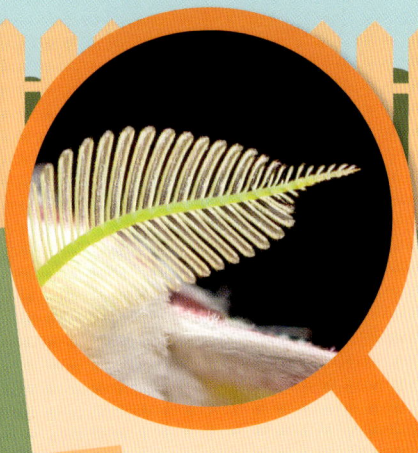

1
- I have two fuzzy antennae on my head.
- I can smell a female moth 11 km (6.8 miles) away.

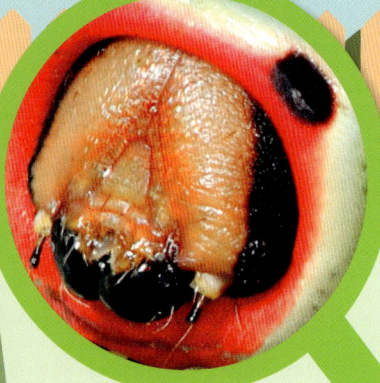

2
- I rear up my colourful head when threatened.
- My tails have pink ends.

3
- I build nests by weaving together leaves.
- I carry a larva in my jaws to make it produce silk.

4
- I roll a perfect ball of dung and bury it.
- My larvae eat the dung.

5
- I am orange in colour.
- I guard my eggs to protect them from predators.

6
- I store nectar in my huge tummy.
- I vomit it up to feed it to other ants in my colony.

7
- In my underwater home, I weave a web and fill it with air.
- This is my personal air supply!

8
- I am found in forests across North America.
- The "eyes" on my wings may confuse predators.

9
- I have seven eyes on my head.
- I use the big eyes on top of my head to look for a mate.

10
- You might confuse me for a flower.
- I am named after this flower.

Answers: 1.Indian moon moth 2.Puss moth caterpillar 3.Weaver ant 4.Dung beetle 5.Cotton harlequin bug 6.Honeypot ant 7.Diving bell spider 8.Polyphemus moth 9.Small spurwing mayfly 10.Orchid mantis

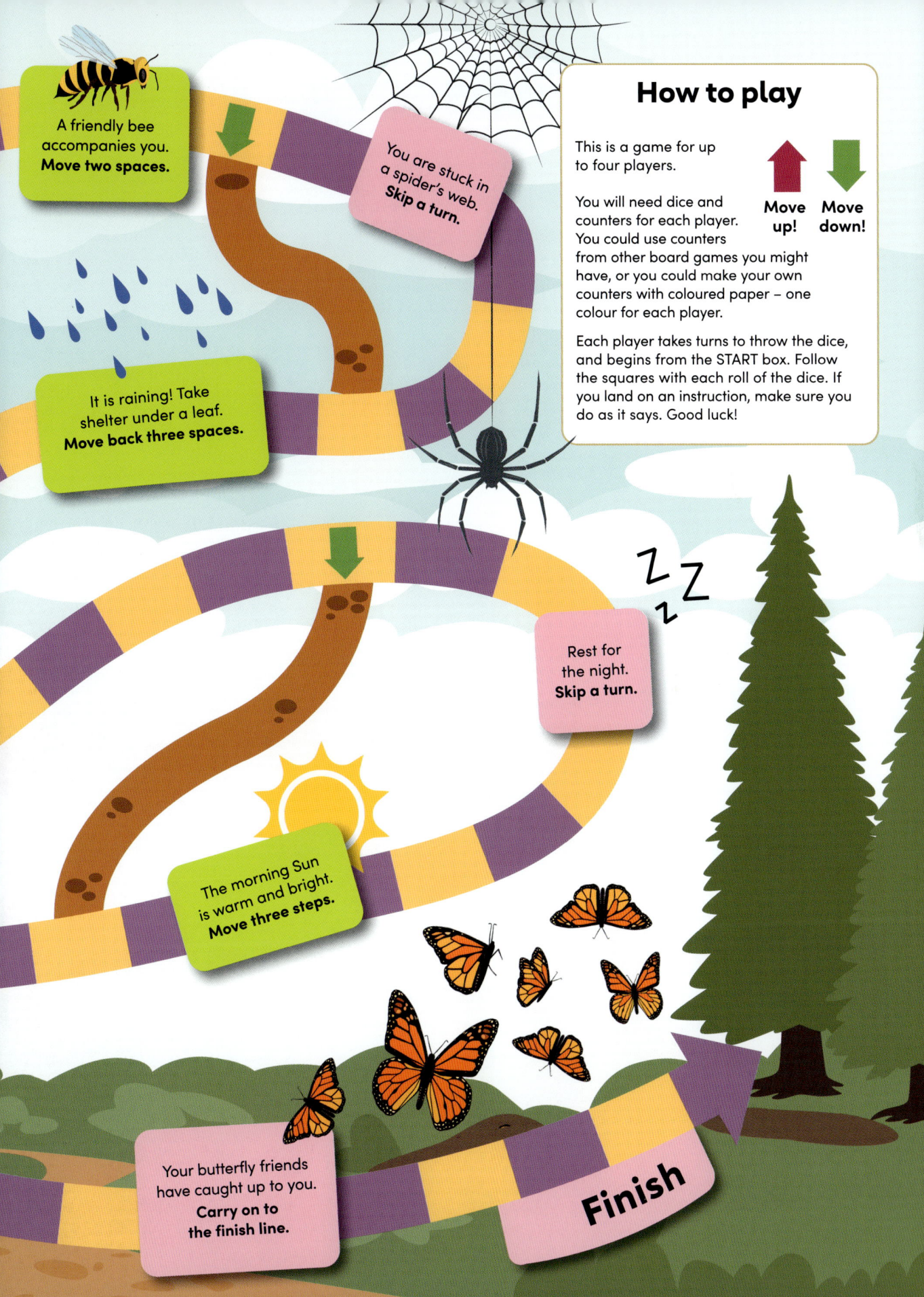

Glossary

Abdomen The rear part of an insect's or spider's body.

Antenna A delicate feeler on an insect, used to smell, touch, or hear.

Arthropod An animal with jointed legs and a body divided into segments, covered by a hard outer skeleton.

Bug Another name for some kinds of arthropods such as insects, spiders, and centipedes.

Camouflage Colours or patterns that help animals to blend into their surroundings.

Colony A group of animals that live and work together.

Compost Rotting plants and leaves.

Crop A plant that is grown and harvested by people.

Dew Moisture that forms on cool surfaces overnight.

Disease An illness that can cause sickness or death.

Disguise Changing the way you look, to look like something else.

Fangs Sharp mouthparts used for injecting venom.

Fungus Living things that reproduce using spores (tiny, special seedlike cells).

Insect A type of arthropod with three body parts and six legs.

Jet propulsion Expelling water (or air) backwards to move forwards.

Larva Young form of an insect.

Metamorphosis A change from immature young to adult form in which the young looks different to the adult.

Microscope An instrument used for looking at very small objects.

Mucus A slimy substance.

Nectar A sweet liquid found in many flowers.

Parasitic A life form that lives on or in another life form, and obtains food from it.

Pest An animal that attacks or destroys things, including crops.

Pollen Tiny grains that join with a plant's egg to make seeds.

Pollination When pollen is transferred to a flower of a female plant, to fertilize it and make seeds.

Predator An animal that hunts other animals for food.

Prey An animal that is hunted by other animals as food.

Proboscis Long tubelike mouthpart for sucking.

Pupa The hard case some young insects change shape inside during metamorphosis.

Saliva A watery liquid in the mouth of an animal that helps to begin digestion.

Sensors Body parts that pick up changes in the body or in the bug's surroundings.

Snout An animal's nose and mouth.

Subtropical Places near tropical areas with warm to hot summers and mild winters.

Swarm A large mass of flying bugs.

Thorax A body part between an insect's head and abdomen.

Tropical Areas near the Equator, with warm, wet climates.

Undergrowth Thickly growing plants and shrubs, often in woodland.

Web A structure of thin silk threads, spun by spiders.

Animal alphabet

Every animal pictured in this book is listed here in alphabetical order. Use the page numbers to find them.

Acorn weevil 15
A small beetle that feeds on growing acorns.

Adanson's house jumper 35
A small jumping spider that often lives in homes in warm parts of the world.

Aphid 26
A tiny insect that feeds on plant sap.

Assassin bug 12
A type of bug that injects saliva to dissolve the insides of its prey.

Backswimmer 32
An insect that swims upside-down on its back, just below the water surface.

Black and orange millipede 6
A flat-bodied millipede with a black body and orange markings.

Bombardier beetle 18
A beetle that sprays a hot chemical to ward off predators.

Caddis fly 32
A mothlike fly whose larvae build protective tubes around their bodies.

Cape burrowing scorpion 30
A large scorpion that digs underground burrows.

Cat flea 6
A parasite found on pet cats.

Cave cricket 10
A type of cricket found in caves, or damp, cool areas.

Cave glow-worm 37
An insect whose larvae live on cave ceilings in New Zealand, using strings of glowing mucus to catch their prey.

Cockroach 34
One of the world's largest and most common pests in homes.

Colorado potato beetle 44
A beetle that feeds on potato crops, making it a pest.

Common pond skater 32
An insect that skims across the surface of the water.

Common red soldier beetle 9
A red-bodied beetle that eats garden pests.

Costa Rican red-leg tarantula 29
A large spider from the rainforests of Central America.

Cotton harlequin bug 20
A colourful shield bug that can have different colours and patterns.

Crane fly 9
A type of flying insect with long, slender legs.

Cuckoo wasp 39
A jewel-coloured wasp that lays its eggs in other insects' nests.

Darkling beetle 31
A type of small, black or brown beetle common in deserts.

Desert locust 22, 40–41
A locust that forms huge swarms, which can destroy entire crops.

Diving bell spider 33
A spider that lives underwater, breathing from an air bubble.

Dragonfly 33, 45
A type of insect with two pairs of clear and lightweight wings, big eyes, and a long body.

Dung beetle 42
A type of beetle that eats dung and lays its eggs in it.

Dusky birch sawfly 14
A dark-coloured insect that feeds on birch trees.

Earwig 43
An insect with pincers at the rear of its body.

Eastern tiger swallowtail 11
A yellow and black butterfly that is common in eastern North America.

Elephant hawk moth 37
One of Europe and Asia's most colourful moths, with olive green and pink wings.

Emerald jewel wasp 30
A shiny green parasitic wasp.

False tiger moth 6–7
A large moth with yellow and black wings.

Flat dark beetle 45
A red, yellow, or brown beetle that eats some insects that feed on wood.

Giraffe weevil 39
A weevil with an unusually long neck.

Goliath beetle 4
A colossal beetle, among the largest insects in the world.

Great diving beetle 12
A large diving beetle that lives in ponds and slow-moving water.

Great green bush-cricket 11
A large green cricket that lives in trees and grasslands.

Green tiger beetle 7
A metallic green beetle that hunts spiders, ants, and caterpillars.

Grey cracker butterfly 17
A butterfly with grey, white, and black patterns that makes a clicking sound as it flies.

Harvester ant 44
A large North American ant that collects seeds for food.

Honeybee 24–25, 45
A bee that lives in colonies, making honey to feed its young.

Honeypot ant 31
An ant that stores liquid food inside its swollen body.

House dust mite 35
A tiny bug that lives in our homes, feeding on dead skin cells.

Ice crawler 31
A type of slow-moving insect that lives in cold environments.

Indian moon moth 11
A large pale moth that flies mainly at night.

Indian tiger centipede 5
A brightly coloured orange-and-black striped centipede with a painful bite.

Itch mite 40
A tiny bug that burrows under human skin.

Ithomiine butterfly 8
A type of butterfly with transparent wings.

Japanese firefly 36
A beetle that glows in the dark.

Jewel bug 5
A small shiny shield bug with bright colours and patterns.

Leaf-cutter ant 15
An ant that cuts slices of leaves and carries them back to its nest, to grow fungus on.

Leaf-mimic katydid 16–17
A type of insect that looks almost exactly like leaves.

Lime butterfly 22
A butterfly that lays its eggs on citrus trees.

Madagascan moon moth 28
A rainforest moth with huge wings and long, flowing tail streamers.

Maggot 42
The larva of a fly, before it becomes an adult.

Marmalade hoverfly 8
A hoverfly with a black-banded orange body.

Meadow grasshopper 7
A green grasshopper that lives in gardens and meadows.

Mexican red-knee tarantula 4
A spider with a striking black and orange pattern.

Monarch butterfly 8, 19
A butterfly that undertakes an epic migration across North America.

Mosquito 40
A type of flying insect. Female mosquitoes can spread diseases such as malaria when they bite.

Net-casting spider 36
A spider that throws a silken web over its prey.

Orchid mantis 16
A praying mantis with pink and white colours, like orchid flowers.

Painted lady butterfly 14
A butterfly with orange-brown, black, and white wings.

Parasitic wasp 21
A type of wasp that feeds on other insects and bugs, killing its hosts.

Pearly green lacewing 8
An insect with a green body and delicate, see-through wings.

Pink-spotted lady beetle 44
A pink-coloured beetle that feeds on pest insects.

Polyphemus moth 19
One of North America's largest moths, with a thick, furry body.

Praying mantis 13, 16
A type of hunting insect that holds its forelegs in a "praying" position, then pounces on passing insects.

Puss moth 18
A moth with fluffy grey hair, which looks a bit like a cat's fur.

Red ant 43
A type of ant with a red-coloured body.

Red spider mite 41
A tiny bug that damages plants.

Sexton beetle 43
A type of beetle that buries small animal bodies to feed its young.

Shield bug 21
A type of bug with a wide flat body, shaped like a shield.

Silverfish 22, 34
A wingless insect that moves a little like a fish.

Small spurwing mayfly 10
A small mayfly with two tails.

Sphinx hawk moth 18
A type of moth that is among the fastest flying insects.

Spiny devil bush-cricket 38
A large cricket with sharp spines all over its body and legs.

Stalk-eyed fly 39
A type of fly with eyes that stick out from its head on long stalks.

Stick insect 17
A type of insect with a body that looks like a twig or branch.

Tanzanian blue ring-legged centipede 13
A centipede with blue legs and a venomous bite.

Termite 26
A type of social insect that lives in colonies and eats wood.

Tick 41
A type of bug that feeds on blood and can spread diseases.

Treehopper 17
A type of tiny insect with unusually shaped, often triangular, plates on its back.

Viceroy butterfly 19
An orange-and-black butterfly that tastes bad to predators.

Vietnamese giant centipede 29
One of the world's largest and most dangerous centipedes.

Wasp 25, 30, 39
A striped flying insect that stings.

Weaver ant 26–27
An ant that builds nests by weaving leaves together.

Wētā 19
A type of large flightless cricket found in New Zealand.

Wolf spider 20
A type of ground-living spider that hunts prey without using webs.

Index

AB
antennae 10, 11
ants 15, 26–27, 31, 43, 44
aphids 26
arthropods 4
assassin bugs 12
babies 20–21
backswimmers 32
bees 24–25
beetles 4, 7, 9, 18
  diet 42–43, 44, 45
  habitats 12, 31, 36
bug-eating plants 15
bush-crickets (katydids) 11, 16–17
butterflies 8, 11, 17, 19
  see also caterpillars

CDE
caddis flies 32
camouflage 16–19
caterpillars 6–7, 14, 18, 21
  metamorphosis 22–23
centipedes 5, 13, 29
cockroaches 30, 34
colonies 26–27, 43
compost 47
crane flies 9
crickets 7, 10, 19, 38
desert bugs 30–31
disguises 17, 18–19
dragonflies 8, 33, 45
dung beetles 42–43
earwigs 43
eggs 20–21

FGHIJ
feelers (antennae) 10, 11
fireflies 36
fleas 6
flies 8, 10, 32, 39
flowers 25, 46
forest bugs 28–29
gardens 46–47
glow-worms 37
grasshoppers 7, 13, 15
groups 24–27, 43
harlequin bugs 20
honey 24, 25
house bugs 34–35
hoverflies 8
ice crawlers 31
jewel bugs 5

KLMN
katydids (bush-crickets) 11, 16–17
lacewings 8
lady beetles 44
locusts 22, 40–41
maggots 42
mayflies 10
meat-eating bugs 12–13
metamorphosis 22–23
millipedes 5, 6
mites 35, 40, 41
mosquitoes 40, 45
moths 11, 19, 28–29, 37
  see also caterpillars
myriapods 5
nests (colonies) 26–27, 43
night bugs 13, 36–37, 46
nymphs 22, 23

PRS
pests 40–41
plant-eating bugs 14–15
pollen 25, 45, 46
pond skaters 32
praying mantises 13, 16
rainforest bugs 28–29
scorpions 4, 30
senses 10–11
shield bugs 21
silverfish 22, 34–35
spiders 4, 20, 29, 35
  webs 13, 33, 36
stalk-eyed flies 39
stick insects 17

TW
tarantulas 4, 29
termites 26
ticks 41
treehoppers 17
true bugs 5, 12, 20, 21
wasps 21, 25, 30, 39
water bugs 12, 32–33
weevils 15, 39
wētās 19

Acknowledgments

DK would like to thank the following people for their help with making the book: Lizzie Munsey for text contributions; Abhijit Dutta, Roohi Sehgal, and Rupa Rao for editorial assistance; Rakesh Kumar for jacket support; Vijay Kandwal for Hires work; Samrajkumar S for picture research administration; Caroline Stamps for proofreading; and Elizabeth Wise for indexing.

The publisher would like to thank the following for their kind permission to reproduce their photographs:

(Key: a-above; b-below/bottom; c-centre; f-far; l-left; r-right; t-top)

1 Getty Images / iStock: Yod67. **3 Alamy Stock Photo:** Nature Picture Library / Bence Mate (b). **4 Dreamstime.com:** Ernest Cooper (tl). **Getty Images / iStock:** Pets-In-Frames (bl). **Shutterstock.com:** SC Hendriks (cr). **4–5 Alamy Stock Photo:** Blickwinkel / B. Trapp (ca). **5 Dreamstime.com:** Utkarsh Patil (b). **6 Dreamstime.com:** Ezumeimages (tl). **naturepl.com:** Stephen Dalton (b). **6–7 Getty Images / iStock:** Yod67. **7 Alamy Stock Photo:** Minden Pictures / Stephen Dalton (tc). **Dreamstime.com:** Alexander Potapov (bl). **8 Alamy Stock Photo:** Biosphoto / Sylvain Cordier (br); Imagebroker.com GmbH & Co. Kg / Arco Images / Schoenberger, A. (cr). **Shutterstock.com:** SuperZiemia (cla). **8–9 Alamy Stock Photo:** Avalon.red / Stephen Dalton (tc). **9 Alamy Stock Photo:** Imagebroker.com / Andre Skonieczny (c, br); Nature Photographers Ltd / Paul R. Sterry (tc/tr). **10 Alamy Stock Photo:** Imagebroker.com / Matthias Lenke (bl); Wild Places Photography / Chris Howes (c). **10–11 Alamy Stock Photo:** Nature Picture Library / Lynn M. Stone (bc). **11 Alamy Stock Photo:** Nature Picture Library / Alex Hyde (tl); Nature Picture Library / MYN / Paul van Hoof (cra). **12 Alamy Stock Photo:** Biosphoto / Stephane Vitzthum (b); Jürgen Kottmann (tr). **13 Shutterstock.com:** FullFrame02 (tr); I Wayan Sumatika (c). **14 Alamy Stock Photo:** Barrie Harwood (ca); Nature Picture Library / Lorraine Bennery (l). **14–15 Alamy Stock Photo:** Barrie Harwood (tc). **15 Alamy Stock Photo:** Minden Pictures / Daniel Heuclin (cra); Nature Picture Library / Alex Hyde (cla); Nature Picture Library / Bence Mate (b). **16 Alamy Stock Photo:** Minden Pictures / Michael & Patricia Fogden (t). **16–17 naturepl.com:** Alex Hyde (bc). **17 Alamy Stock Photo:** Minden Pictures / Wahrmut Sobainsky / NiS (cla); RGB Ventures / SuperStock / Christina L. Evans / Rainbow (c). **Dreamstime.com:** Carlos Soler Martinez (t). **18 Alamy Stock Photo:** Amazon-Images (tl). **Depositphotos Inc:** Vblinov (b). **naturepl.com:** Nature Production (cr). **19 Alamy Stock Photo:** Grant Heilman Photography / Runk / Schoenberger (br); Stockimo / Hotgranny (tl). **Shutterstock.com:** Chris Moody (c). **20 Alamy Stock Photo:** Ben Nottidge (tl). **naturepl.com:** Alex Hyde (cr). **20–21 naturepl.com:** Nature Production (b). **21 Alamy Stock Photo:** Nature Picture Library / Lucas Bustamante (tr). **22 Alamy Stock Photo:** Frank Hecker (clb). **Dreamstime.com:** Shariqkhan (tl). **Getty Images / iStock:** Tomasz Klejdysz (bl). **22–23 Dreamstime.com:** Sutisa Kangvansap. **Science Photo Library:** Claude Nuridsany & Marie Perennou (b); Wirestock (l). **25 Alamy Stock Photo:** Imagebroker.com / Frank Derer (bc); Evan Bowen-Jones (t); James Schutte (cl). **26 Alamy Stock Photo:** Hemis / Garcia Julien (bl). **Dreamstime.com:** Edward Phillips (tr). **Shutterstock.com:** Frank60 (br). **27 Alamy Stock Photo:** Blickwinkel / K. Wothe. **28–29 naturepl.com:** Nick Garbutt (t). **Shutterstock.com:** Vince Adam (cb). **29 naturepl.com:** Alex Hyde (br). **30 Alamy Stock Photo:** Nature Picture Library / Jen Guyton; Nature Picture Library / Emanuele Biggi (tr). **31 Alamy Stock Photo:** John Cancalosi (tr); Martin Harvey (cla); Minden Pictures / Piotr Naskrecki (br). **32 Alamy Stock Photo:** Minden Pictures / Stephen Dalton (b); Nick Upton (ca). **naturepl.com:** Jan Hamrsky (tr). **33 Alamy Stock Photo:** Blickwinkel / H. Bellmann / F. Hecker (t); Ian West (bl). **34 Alamy Stock Photo:** Nigel Cattlin (bl). **Depositphotos Inc:** Leonid_Eremeychuk (cla). **34–35 Alamy Stock Photo:** Rob Whitworth (tc). **35 123RF.com:** eraxion (cl). **Depositphotos Inc:** Jacek_Kadaj (cra). **Dreamstime.com:** Viniciussouza06 (br). **36 Alamy Stock Photo:** Nature Picture Library / Nick Garbutt (tl). **Getty Images:** Moment / Ali Majdfar (c). **36–37 Minden Pictures:** Hiroya Minakuchi (b). **37 Alamy Stock Photo:** Malcolm Schuyl (t); Markus Thomenius (c). **Dreamstime.com:** Mathiasrhode (tl). **38 Alamy Stock Photo:** Imagebroker.com / Guenter Fischer. **39 Alamy Stock Photo:** Nature Picture Library / Alex Hyde (t). **Getty Images / iStock:** Jojo Dexter (tr). **Getty Images:** Moment Open / Adegsm (bl). **40 Alamy Stock Photo:** Gado Images / Smith Collection / James Gathany (tr). **Getty Images:** AFP / Yasuyoshi Chiba (cr). **Science Photo Library:** Kent Wood (cl). **40–41 Getty Images:** AFP / Yasuyoshi Chiba (b). **41 Getty Images:** AFP / Yasuyoshi Chiba (t). **Shutterstock.com:** BirdShutterB (tr). **Shutterstock.com:** Irin-K (cla). **42 Dreamstime.com:** Steve Mann (tl). **42–43 Alamy Stock Photo:** VWPics / Sergio Pitamitz (b). **43 Alamy Stock Photo:** Andrew Newman Nature Pictures (tr); Imagebroker.com / Bob Gibbons (l). **Dreamstime.com:** Triwidana (b). **44–45 Alamy Stock Photo:** Grant Heilman Photography / Runk / Schoenberger (tc); Minden Pictures / Mark Moffett (b). **45 Alamy Stock Photo:** Nature Picture Library / Kim Taylor (ca). **Dreamstime.com:** Lirtlon (cr). **Shutterstock.com:** Husmubarr (bc). **46 Dreamstime.com:** Vlue (cb). **Getty Images:** Moment / Jacky Parker Photography (bc). **naturepl.com:** Ernie Janes (cb). **47 Dreamstime.com:** Graham Corney (c). **Getty Images:** Moment / Athima Tongloom (tc). **Shutterstock.com:** BernadetteB (bc). **48–49 Dreamstime.com:** Rinat Sultanov (Acorn). **50 Alamy Stock Photo:** Blickwinkel / K. Wothe (tr); Nature Picture Library / Alex Hyde (cla); VWPics / Sergio Pitamitz (cb); Ben Nottidge (crb). **Depositphotos Inc:** Vblinov (ca). **51 Alamy Stock Photo:** Blickwinkel / H. Bellmann / F. Hecker (tc); John Cancalosi (tr); Imagebroker.com / Matthias Lenke (c); Minden Pictures / Michael & Patricia Fogden (cr); Stockimo / Hotgranny (clb). **52 Getty Images / iStock:** Taras Dubov (cr); Kusni Ah (cb); Nadiia Romanchenko (crb). **Shutterstock.com:** Akbaly (ca); Alfmaler (bl). **53 Dreamstime.com:** Kharlamova (cb). **Shutterstock.com:** Akbaly (bc). **54 Alamy Stock Photo:** Biosphoto / Sylvain Cordier (b).

Cover images: *Front:* **Alamy Stock Photo:** Blickwinkel / B. Trapp cr. **Dreamstime.com:** Alexstar bc, Kristof Degreef tr, Dibrova cla / (Caterpillar), EPhotocorp cb, Domiciano Pablo Romero Franco tl, Mark Higgins cra, Isselee cb / (Mantis), Johan007 ca / (Wasp), Lukas Jonaitis cl / (Caterpillar), Mattwatt c, MorganOliver cra / (Bedbug), Herlinde Noppe crb, Xunbin Pan cra / (Cicada), cl, Ryan Pike ca, Takepicsforfun cb / (Lantern Fly), Dmitry Zhukov tc. **Getty Images / iStock:** Antagain br. **Shutterstock.com:** Grafvision cla; *Back:* **Alamy Stock Photo:** Amazon-Images tl, Larry Doherty crb, Minden Pictures / Mitsuhiko Immamori tr / (Silk Moth), Nature Picture Library / Kim Taylor tr, PjrStudio cra. **Depositphotos Inc:** Alex.Stemmer clb. **Dorling Kindersley:** Frank Greenaway / Natural History Museum, London cr. **Dreamstime.com:** Marcouliana br, Subbotina bl, Verastuchelova cl. **Getty Images / iStock:** Darkdiamond67 cla. **naturepl.com:** Hans Christoph Kappel tl / (Spider). **Shutterstock.com:** Irin-K cra / (Bee), Anton Kozyrev tc; *Spine:* **Getty Images:** Moment / Jasius.